Pebble® Plus

ICE AGE ANIMALS

Ancient Armadillos

by Jeni Wittrock

Consulting Editor: Gail Saunders-Smith, PhD

Content Consultant: Margaret M. Yacobucci, PhD
Education and Outreach Coordinator,
Paleontological Society; Associate Professor,
Department of Geology, Bowling Green State University

Raintree is an imprint of Capstone Global Library Limited, a company incorporated in England and Wales having its registered office at 7 Pilgrim Street, London, EC4V 6LB – Registered company number: 6695582

www.raintree.co.uk
myorders@raintree.co.uk

Text © Capstone Global Library Limited 2015
The moral rights of the proprietor have been asserted.

Editorial Credits
Peggie Carley and Janet Kusmierski, designers; Wanda Winch, media researcher; Laura Manthe, production specialist

ISBN 978 1 4062 9369 2 (hardback)
18 17 16 15 14
10 9 8 7 6 5 4 3 2 1

ISBN 978 1 4062 9376 0 (paperback)
19 18 17 16
10 9 8 7 6 5 4 3 2 1

British Library Cataloguing in Publication Data
A full catalogue record for this book is available from the British Library.

Photo Credits
Illustrator: Jon Hughes.
Shutterstock: Alex Staroseltsev, snowball, April Cat, icicles,
Leigh Prather, ice crystals, pcruciatti, winter background

Printed and bound in China.

Contents

Tales of giants 4

Tough armour 10

Baby armadillos 16

Changing times 18

Glossary..................................22

Read more 23

Websites 23

Index 24

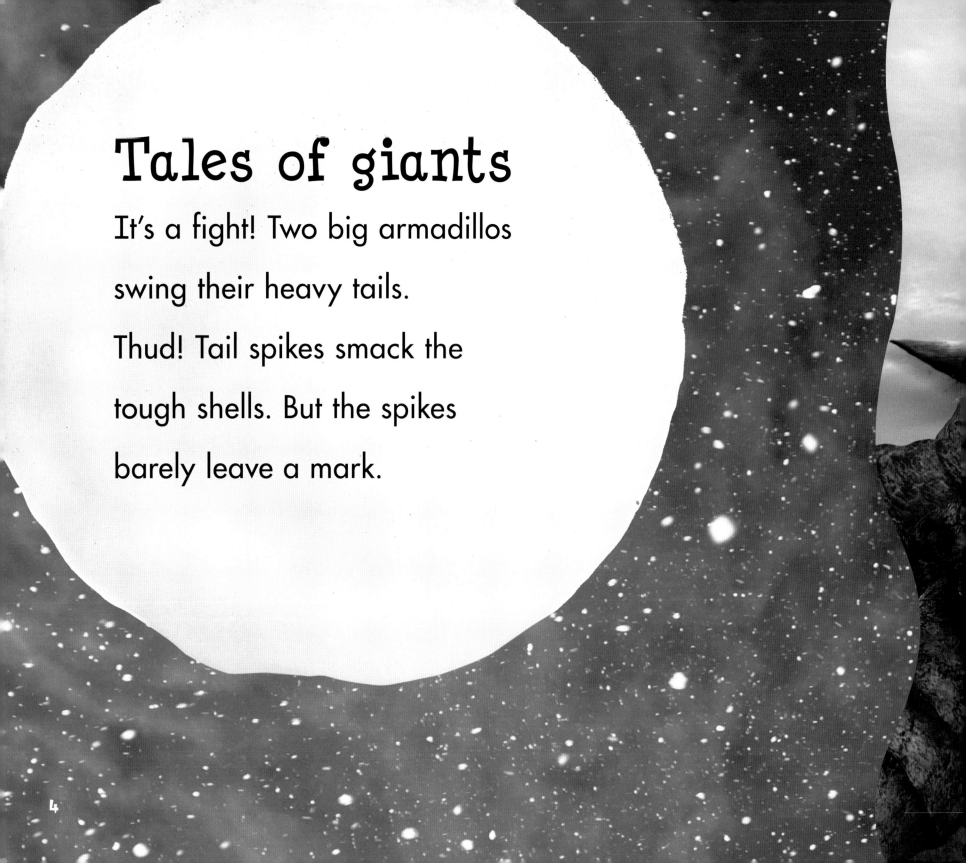

Tales of giants

It's a fight! Two big armadillos swing their heavy tails. Thud! Tail spikes smack the tough shells. But the spikes barely leave a mark.

4

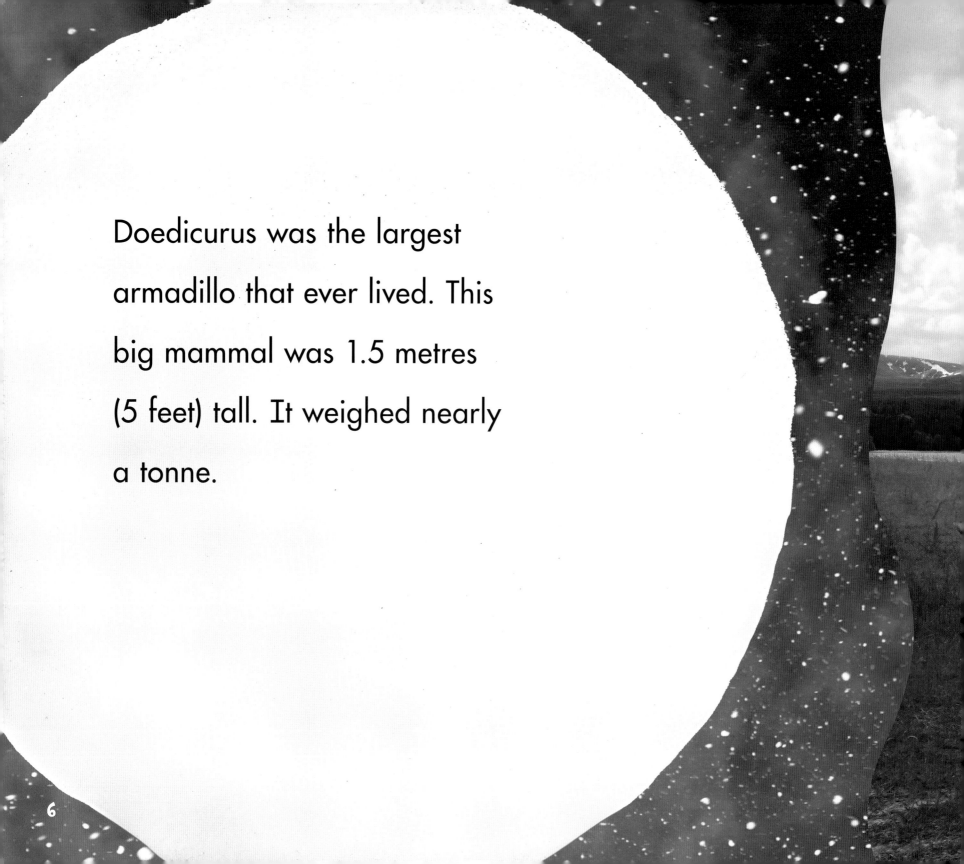

Doedicurus was the largest armadillo that ever lived. This big mammal was 1.5 metres (5 feet) tall. It weighed nearly a tonne.

These creatures roamed North and South America long ago. Ancient armadillos grazed in grasslands and woodlands during the Ice Age.

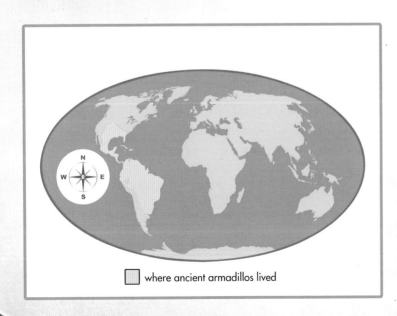

where ancient armadillos lived

Tough armour

Ancient armadillos had brown-grey bodies. Their shells were made up of bony scales called scutes. Tough scales covered armadillos' heads, too.

The armadillos had short legs and moved slowly. Their bumpy teeth were perfect for chewing grass and other plants. Spikes topped the ends of their tails.

The armadillos looked tough, but they did not hunt other animals. Their strong armour protected them from predators such as sabretooth cats.

Baby armadillos

Like armadillos today, ancient armadillos were mammals. A young Doedicurus stayed with its mother. She fed and protected her baby.

Changing times

Over time, Earth warmed up. Life became hard for the armadillos. The plants they ate died off. More predators hunted the armadillos.

Doedicurus became extinct
about 10,000 years ago.
Today's sloths and armadillos
are their relatives.

Glossary

armour protective covering

extinct no longer living; an extinct animal is one that has died out, with no more of its kind

graze eat grass and low plants

Ice Age time when much of Earth was covered in ice; the last ice age ended about 11,500 years ago

mammal warm–blooded animal

mate join together to make young

predator animal that hunts other animals for food

protect keep safe

relative part of the same family

scute one of many tough, plate-like scales that cover and protect an animal's body

smack hit

spike sharp, horn-like body part

Read more

First Encyclopedia of Dinosaurs and Prehistoric Life
(Usborne First Encyclopedias), Sam Taplin (Usborne
Publishing Ltd, 2011)

The Ice Age Tracker's Guide, Adrian Lister and
Martin Ursell (Frances Lincoln Children's Books, 2010)

A Weekend With Dinosaurs (Fantasy Field Trips),
Claire Throp (Raintree, 2014)

Websites

www.bbc.co.uk/nature/prehistoric
All you need to know about prehistoric life!

www.nhm.ac.uk/kids-only/dinosaurs
Find out everything you need to know about prehistoric
life. Look at 3-D dinosaurs, learn fun facts, play games,
and take a quiz!

Index

armour 14

babies 16
bodies 10

colour 10

extinct 20

fighting 4
food 12 18

grazing 8

head 10
homes 8

Ice Age 8

legs 12

mammals 16
mothers 16

predators 14 18

sabretooth cats 14
scales 10
scutes 10
shells 4 10
size 6
sloths 20
speed 12, 14
spikes 4, 12

tail 4 12
teeth 12